16-19
MATHEMATICS

Foundations

Unit Guide

The School Mathematics Project

10.

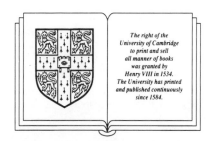

The right of the
University of Cambridge
to print and sell
all manner of books
was granted by
Henry VIII in 1534.
The University has printed
and published continuously
since 1584.

Cambridge University Press

Cambridge   New York   Port Chester   Melbourne   Sydney

Main authors   Simon Baxter
                        Stan Dolan
                        Doug French
                        Andy Hall
                        Barrie Hunt
                        Lorna Lyons

Team leader   Barrie Hunt

Project director   Stan Dolan

Published by the Press Syndicate of the University of Cambridge
The Pitt Building, Trumpington Street, Cambridge CB2 1RP
40 West 20th Street, New York, NY 10011–4211, USA
10 Stamford Road, Oakleigh, Melbourne 3166, Australia

© Cambridge University Press 1991

First published 1991

Produced by Gecko Limited, Bicester, Oxon

Cover Design by Iguana Creative Design

Printed in Great Britain at the University Press, Cambridge

The authors would like to give special thanks to Ann White for
her help in producing the trial edition and in preparing this book
for publication.

British Library cataloguing in publication data
16–19 mathematics.
Foundations. Unit guide
1. Mathematics.
I. School Mathematics Project
510

ISBN 0 521 40879 2

Contents

Introduction to 16–19 Mathematics

Nobody reads introductions and nobody reads teachers' guides, so what chance does the introduction to this Unit Guide have? The least we can do is to keep it short! We hope that you will find the discussion point and tasksheet commentaries and ideas on presentation and enrichment useful.

The School Mathematics Project was founded in 1961 with the purpose of improving the teaching of mathematics in schools by the provision of new course materials. SMP authors are experienced teachers and each new venture is tested by schools in a draft version before publication. Work on *16–19 Mathematics* started in 1986 and the pilot of the course has been used by over 30 schools since 1987.

Since its inception the SMP has always offered an 'after sales service' for teachers using its materials. If you have any comments on *16–19 Mathematics*, or would like advice on its use, please write to:

> 16–19 Mathematics
> The SMP Office
> The University
> Southampton SO9 5NH

Why 16–19 Mathematics?

A major problem in mathematics education is how to enable ordinary mortals to comprehend in a few years concepts which geniuses have taken centuries to develop. In theory, our view of how to pass on this body of knowledge effectively and pleasurably has changed considerably; but no great revolution in practice has been seen in sixth-form classrooms generally. We hope that in this course, the change in approach to mathematics teaching embodied in GCSE schemes will be carried forward. The principles applied in the course are appropriate to this aim.

- Students are actively involved in developing mathematical ideas.
- Premature abstraction and over-reliance on algorithms are avoided.
- Wherever possible, problems arise from, or at least relate to, everyday life.
- Appropriate use is made of modern technology such as graphic calculators and microcomputers.
- Misunderstandings are confronted and acted upon.
  By applying these principles and presenting material in an attractive way, A level mathematics is made more accessible to students and more meaningful to them as individuals. The *16–19 Mathematics* course is flexible enough to provide for the whole range of students who obtain at least a grade C at GCSE.

Structure of the courses

The A and AS level courses have a core-plus-options structure. Details of the full range of possibilities, including A and AS level *Further Mathematics* courses, may be obtained from the Joint Matriculation Board, Manchester M15 6EU.

For the A level course *Mathematics (Pure with Applications)*, students must study eight core units and a further two optional units. The structure diagram below shows how the units are related to each other. Other optional units are being developed to give students an opportunity to study aspects of mathematics which are appropriate to their personal interests and enthusiasms.

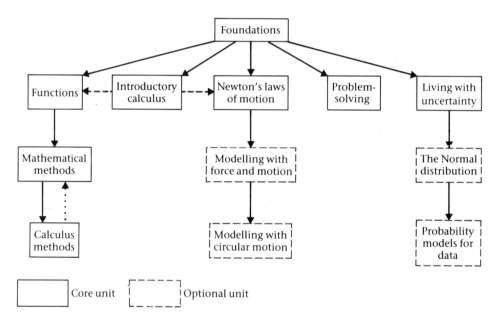

The *Foundations* unit should be started before or at the same time as any other core unit.

Any of the other units can be started at the same time as the *Foundations* unit. The second half of *Functions* requires prior coverage of *Introductory calculus*. *Newton's laws of motion* requires calculus notation which is covered in the initial chapters of *Introductory calculus*.

The Polynomial approximations chapter in *Mathematical methods* requires prior coverage of some sections of *Calculus methods*.

For the AS level *Mathematics (Pure with Applications)* course, students must study *Foundations*, *Introductory calculus* and *Functions*. Students must then study a further two applied units.

Material

In traditional mathematics texts the theory has been written in a didactic manner for passive reading, in the hope that it will be accepted and understood – or, more realistically, that the teacher will supply the necessary motivation and deal with problems of understanding. In marked contrast, *16–19 Mathematics* adopts a questing mode, demanding the active participation of students. The textbooks contain several new devices to aid a more active style of learning.

- Topics are opened up through **group discussion points**, signalled in the text by the symbol

and enclosed in rectangular frames. These consist of pertinent questions to be discussed by students, with guidance and help from the teacher. Commentaries for discussion points are included in this unit guide.

- The text is also punctuated by **thinking points**, having the shape

and again containing questions. These should be dealt with by students without the aid of the teacher. In facing up to the challenge offered by the thinking points it is intended that students will achieve a deeper insight and understanding. A solution within the text confirms or modifies the student's response to each thinking point.

- At appropriate points in the text, students are referred to **tasksheets** which are placed at the end of the relevant chapter. These mostly consist of a self-contained piece of work which is used to investigate a concept prior to any formal exposition. In many cases, it takes up an idea raised in a discussion point, examining it in more detail and preparing the way for formal treatment. There are also **extension tasksheets** (labelled by an E) for higher attaining students which investigate a topic in more depth and **supplementary tasksheets** (labelled by an S) which are intended to help students with a relatively weak background in a particular topic. Commentaries for all the tasksheets are included in this unit guide.

The aim of the **exercises** is to check full understanding of principles and give the student confidence through reinforcement of his or her understanding.

Graphic calculators/microcomputers are used throughout the course. In particular, much use is made of graph plotters. The use of videos and equipment for practical work is also recommended.

As well as the textbooks and unit guides, there is a *Teacher's resource file*. This file contains:

- review sheets which may be used for homework or tests;

- datasheets;

- technology datasheets which give help with using particular calculators or pieces of software;

- a programme of worksheets for more able students which would, in particular, help prepare them for the STEP examination.

Introduction to the unit (for the teacher)

The *Foundations* unit is fundamental to the *16–19 Mathematics* scheme. As its name implies it introduces ideas that will be built upon in later units. Not only does it cover important content, it also sets the scene for the way in which the whole course will be taught, encouraging:

- discussion of mathematical concepts, both as a class and within groups;
- a facility with technology, through using software packages and/or graph sketching calculators;
- awareness of the value of sketch graphs;
- development of algebraic confidence and competence;
- an ability to read mathematical writing, presented here in the form of 'case studies';
- awareness of ideas of accuracy, including the difference between exact and non-exact solutions to equations.

This list is by no means exhaustive, but it indicates important themes that recur throughout the unit and should be reinforced wherever possible.

Using this unit

Students studying the *Foundations* unit will have an enormous range of backgrounds and abilities. There will be students with GCSE grade C, as well as students with a grade A who may have met some of the material before. As a guide, the following paths through the unit are recommended. The use of tasksheets that are bracketed will depend upon the previous experience of the students.

The mainstream student

Chapter	Tasksheets
1	1, 3, 5, 6
2	1, 2, 3, 4, 5, 8
3	1, 2
4	1, 2, (4S), (5S), 6
5	1, 2

The student with a weaker background

Chapter	Tasksheets
1	1, 2S, 3, 4S, 5, 6, 7S
2	1, 2, 3, (4), 5, 8
3	1, 2
4	1S, 2, 4S, 5S, 6
5	1, 2

The very able student

Chapter	Tasksheets
1	1, 3E, 5E, 6
2	1, 2, 3, 4, 5, 6E, 7E, 8
3	1, 2
4	1, 2, 3E, 6
5	1, 2, 3E

The chapters may be taught sequentially, or, if the unit is taught by two members of staff, a possible division is chapters 1 + 3 and chapters 2 + 4 + 5. Some additional notes on the individual chapters follow.

1 Graphs

In this chapter the student will:

- learn how to use a graph plotting package;
- revise and extend his or her knowledge of straight-line graphs;
- learn how to sketch and interpret quadratic functions;
- learn the technique of completing the square;
- revise the factorisation of quadratic functions.

Following a general introduction to graph sketching, the chapter develops the properties of linear and quadratic functions. The emphasis is on using a graph plotter to motivate the algebraic techniques. Many of the ideas introduced here will be reinforced in later units.

2 Sequences

In this chapter the student will:

- meet a variety of sequences;
- appreciate properties of sequences including periodicity, convergence, oscillation and divergence;
- learn how sequences may be expressed inductively and by using a general term;
- learn to sum arithmetic and geometric series;
- meet applications of series to finance;
- learn how to use sigma notation;
- meet examples of infinite series and discuss the idea of convergence.

Sequences are introduced in the context of financial applications. Ideas of pattern and generalisation are used in the discussion of general sequences before the arithmetic sequence is covered in some detail.

Compound interest, savings schemes and mortgages lead into sigma notation and geometric progressions, culminating with sums of infinite geometric progressions.

3 Functions and graphs

In this chapter the student will:

- learn how to use function notation;
- meet terminology associated with functions including the idea of domain and subsets of the real numbers $\mathbb{R}$ (including $\mathbb{N}$, $\mathbb{Q}$, and $\mathbb{Z}$);
- meet the modulus function;
- use function notation to describe translations of graphs;
- appreciate the reasons for sketching rather than plotting a graph;
- learn to sketch graphs using properties of dominance.

The language of functions recurs throughout the *16–19 Mathematics* course and is developed in this chapter. It is not intended that this should be over-formal, but it is important that students should understand that on occasions domains can play an important role. Function notation is also a useful tool and it is developed later in the chapter in relation to sketching graphs.

4 Expressions and equations

In this chapter the student will:

- discuss algebraic terminology that may have been only partially understood previously;
- learn that letters can be used in algebra in a variety of ways;
- practise formulating equations;
- learn to use the quadratic equation formula;
- learn to choose an appropriate method for solving a quadratic equation;
- appreciate the difference between exact and approximate solutions;
- learn to solve simple polynomial inequalities;
- learn to use the factor theorem to factorise a polynomial.

The theme of this chapter is algebra and the solution of equations, both quadratic and polynomial, via the factor theorem and using exact methods. Students often have trouble with the correct use of algebraic language and notation and this is stressed throughout the chapter.

5 Numerical methods

In this chapter the student will:

- meet numerical techniques for solving equations;
- understand that not all equations may be solved using analytic techniques;
- use sketch graphs to locate the roots of an equation;
- see that iterative formulas may converge, diverge, or converge to an unexpected root.

Part of the philosophy of *16–19 Mathematics* is that numerical techniques should arise naturally throughout the course. It is to be expected that, with the advent of graphical calculators, many students will adopt the process of 'zooming-in' as a natural strategy for the solution of equations.

Tasksheets and resources

This list gives an overview of where tasksheets are to be used. Items in *italics* refer to resources not included in the main text.

1 Graphs

1.1 Introduction
Tasksheet 1 – Investigating curves
Technology datasheet – Plotting graphs
1.2 Linear graphs
Tasksheet 2S – The equation of a straight line
1.3 Quadratic functions
Tasksheet 3 or 3E – Translations of the quadratic curve
1.4 Completing the square
Tasksheet 4S – Multiplying brackets
Tasksheet 5 – Completing the square
Tasksheet 5E – Completing the square (algebraic approach)
1.5 Zeros of quadratics
Tasksheet 6 – Factorised quadratics
1.6 Factorising quadratics
Tasksheet 7S – Further factorisation

2 Sequences

2.1 Sequences in action
2.2 Generating sequences
Tasksheet 1 – Patterns and sequences
Technology datasheet – Repeated calculations
2.3 The general term
Tasksheet 2 – The general term
2.4 Arithmetic series
Tasksheet 3 – Arithmetic series
2.5 Finance
Tasksheet 4 – Annual percentage rate (APR)
Tasksheet 5 – Mortgages
Technology datasheet – Repeated calculations
2.6 Sigma notation
Tasksheet 6E – Using sigma
2.7 Geometric series
Tasksheet 7E – Mortgages revisited
2.8 Infinity
Tasksheet 8 – Zeno's paradox

Equipment/material needed

The only essential resources needed to complement the *Foundations* unit are technology datasheets which can be found in the *Teacher's resource file*. This file also contains various optional worksheets and their commentaries together with full guidance on their use.

1 Graphs

1.1 Introduction

> Suppose the profit is £x per radio.
>
> (a) Find the number of radios that the trader sells per week in terms of x.
>
> (b) What is her total profit from sales in terms of x?
>
> (c) What are the equations of the straight-line graph in example 1 and the graph that you have drawn?

(a) The expression $60 - 10x$ or $10(6 - x)$ can be established fairly easily.

(b) The table was completed by multiplying

'Profit per radio' × 'Number of radios sold'.

The answer given in part (a) leads to

$$x \times (60 - 10x) = x(60 - 10x)$$
$$= 60x - 10x^2$$

or any equivalent expression.

(c) The graph in example 1 shows the number of radios sold at a given profit per radio. If y stands for the number of radios sold, then (a) gives

$$y = 60 - 10x$$

This is the equation of the first graph.

The graph that has been drawn shows the total profit for a given profit per radio. If t stands for the total profit, then (b) gives

$$t = x(60 - 10x)$$

This is the equation of the second graph.

1.2 **Linear functions**

> What assumptions have been made to obtain straight line
> graphs? Do you think these assumptions are reasonable?

'30 miles per day' is such a familiar phrase that it is easy to overlook
the many inaccuracies and assumptions that are inherent in it.

- The walker will have to stop overnight, which would introduce steps
  into the graph.

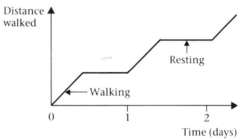

- It is unlikely that his overnight stops will be exactly 30 miles apart.

- There will probably be short rests throughout the day for
  refreshments, introducing more steps into the graph.

- He could not maintain a perfectly constant walking speed. This
  would be affected by hills, terrain, traffic, fatigue and many other
  factors.

Overall, the true graph might look like this:

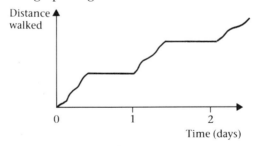

Clearly, it is impractical to take all these factors into consideration –
it would take some very sophisticated equipment to measure and
record every fluctuation, and to plot the graph accurately.

The level of sophistication required will vary, depending on the
purpose for which the information is to be used. A physiologist,
researching into the effects of long-distance walking on the human
body, may require detailed information on the periods of rest and
activity. A journalist is more likely to want an overall picture of the
progress made, and be content with '30 miles per day'.

1.3 Quadratic factors

(a) Use a graph plotter to plot the function

$$y = ax^2$$

for various positive, negative and fractional values of a. What do you notice?

(b) Plot the function

$$y = ax^2 + bx + c$$

for various positive, negative and fractional values of a, b and c. (You will need to vary one coefficient at a time, keeping the others constant.) What do you notice?

The graphs given by the equation

$$y = ax^2 + bx + c \qquad (a \neq 0)$$

have many interesting features but the basic shape remains the same as shown below.

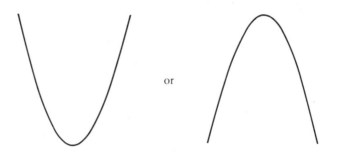

or

Other features and properties which may be observed are

(a) for $y = ax^2$

- similarity of shape;
- symmetry about the line $x = 0$;
- the graph always passes through $(0, 0)$;
- the graph does not cross the x-axis;
- the difference between the cases $a > 0$ and $a < 0$;
- the effect of making a larger and smaller.

(b) for $y = ax^2 + bx + c$

- comparison between the graphs of $y = ax^2$ and $y = ax^2 + bx + c$ for particular values of a;

- symmetry about a different vertical line;

- the cases $b = 0$ and $c = 0$;

- maximum or minimum value;

- the effect of varying a with b and c constant. How does this compare with your findings for $y = ax^2$?

- the effect of varying c with a and b constant.

The effects of varying a, b and c are studied further in the rest of this section.

1.5 Zeros of quadratics

> (a) If a product of two numbers ab equals 0, what can you say about either a or b?
>
> (b) State all solutions of
>
>   (i) $x + 2 = 0$
>
>   (ii) $x - 1 = 0$
>
>   (iii) $(x - 1)(x + 2) = 0$

(a) Notice that $a \times 0 = 0$ whatever the value of a.

Also, $0 \times b = 0$ whatever the value of b.

So $ab = 0$ when either $a = 0$ or $b = 0$.

The converse is also true; i.e. if $ab = 0$ then a or b (or both) must be zero.

(b) (i) $x + 2 = 0$
$$\Rightarrow x = -2$$

    (ii) $x - 1 = 0$
$$\Rightarrow x = 1$$

    (iii) $(x - 1)(x + 2) = 0$
$$\Rightarrow x - 1 = 0 \text{ or } x + 2 = 0$$
$$\Rightarrow \quad x = 1 \quad \text{or} \quad x = -2$$

1.6 **Factorising quadratics**

(a) Explain why $x + 2$ is a possible factor of $x^2 - x - 12$, yet $x - 5$ could not be a factor.

(b) Give all twelve possible factors of $x^2 - x - 12$.

(c) Factorise $x^2 - x - 12$.

(a) If the factors of $x^2 - x - 12$ are $(x + a)(x + b)$ then $ab = -12$. 2 is a factor of -12 whereas 5 is not.

(b) $x \pm 1, x \pm 2, x \pm 3, x \pm 4, x \pm 6, x \pm 12$

(c) $(x - 4)(x + 3)$

Investigating curves

This tasksheet serves two purposes. You will see a variety of graphs, and begin to be aware of some of their features. In the process, you will become familiar with a graph plotter and its capabilities.

This investigation will take time but should not be extended for too long. The questions are intended to help those who are not sure what to do, though you are encouraged to try out variations of the given functions, or to superimpose graphs for comparison.

1 For each graph, you might consider:

- general impression of shape;
- whether or not it passes through the origin;
- steepness of the graph in different places;
- symmetries – reflection, rotation, translation;
- values of x for which the function is undefined;
- what happens when x is close to the undefined values;
- what happens when x is very large (positive or negative);
- whether or not there are any restrictions on the values of y;
- similarities to graphs of other functions;
- how the functions might be classified.

The list is not exhaustive, nor is it necessary for you to record all features at this stage.

2 $y = x$ and $y = x^3$ have rotational symmetry about the origin.
$y = x^2$ and $y = x^4$ have a line of symmetry, the y-axis.
The extension of these properties to higher powers of x should be considered.

3 The graphs are related by reflection in the x-axis.

4 You should notice that they are related by reflection in the line $y = x$.

The equation of a straight line

This tasksheet is intended to introduce or revise the concepts of gradient, intercept and the equation $y = mx + c$.

The tasksheet explains that the equation $y = mx + c$ represents a straight line with gradient m, passing through the point $(0, c)$, the intercept with the y-axis.

As well as noting how to calculate gradient precisely, it should be observed that

- a numerically large gradient means a steeply sloping line;

- a numerically small gradient means a flatter line;

- a gradient of zero means that the line is flat or horizontal (parallel to the x-axis);

- a positive gradient slopes upwards to the right;

- a negative gradient slopes downwards to the right.

1 (a), (b)

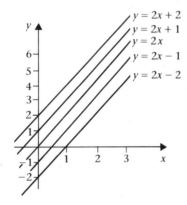

$y = 2x + 2$
$y = 2x + 1$
$y = 2x$
$y = 2x - 1$
$y = 2x - 2$

Varying c translates the line up and down. The value of c is where the line crosses the y-axis.

2 (a), (b)

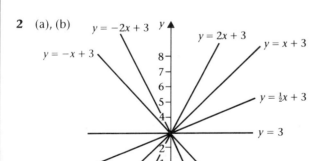

$y = -2x + 3$
$y = -x + 3$
$y = 2x + 3$
$y = x + 3$
$y = \frac{1}{2}x + 3$
$y = 3$

Varying m changes the gradient of the line. When m is positive, the line slopes up as x increases. When m is negative the line slopes down as x increases.

3

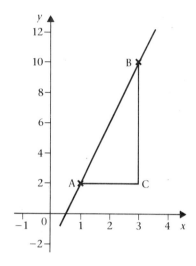

$$\text{Gradient} = \frac{BC}{AC} = \frac{8}{2} = 4$$

4 (a) Gradient = $\dfrac{11 - 2}{2 + 1} = \dfrac{9}{3} = 3$ (b) Gradient = $\dfrac{8}{-4} = -2$

(c) Gradient = $\dfrac{0}{3} = 0$

5 (a) Gradient = $\dfrac{4}{2} = 2$

(b) The line crosses the y-axis at $(0, 1)$ so the y-intercept is 1.

(c) When $x = 0$ When $x = 2$
$\quad\quad y = 2 \times 0 + 1$ $\quad\quad y = 2 \times 2 + 1$
$\quad\quad y = 1$ $\quad\quad y = 5$

(d) For $y = 2x + 1$ 1 represents the y-intercept.

2 represents the gradient.

6 (a) Choose any two points on the line, for example $(-1, 2)$ and $(-3, 8)$, which give the gradient -3.

(b) The line crosses the y-axis at $(0, -1)$, so the y-intercept is -1.

(c) For any point on the line, substituting the x-coordinate in the equation will give the y-coordinate; for example, take the point $(1, -4)$:

When $x = 1$
$$y = -3 \times 1 - 1$$
$$y = -4$$

(d) For $y = -3x - 1$ -1 represents the y-intercept.

-3 represents the gradient.

7 (a) The equation of the line is $y = -2x + 6$

                       gradient y-intercept

(b) The equation of the line is $y = 5x - 2$

                       gradient y-intercept

8 (a) $m = -4, c = 9$

(b) $y = 3x + \frac{3}{2} \Rightarrow m = 3, c = \frac{3}{2}$

(c) $y = 2x + \frac{5}{2} \Rightarrow m = 2, c = \frac{5}{2}$

(d) $y = -\frac{3}{5}x - 2 \Rightarrow m = -\frac{3}{5}, c = -2$

(e) $y = 5x - 7 \Rightarrow m = 5, c = -7$

(f) $m = \frac{1}{3}, c = -\frac{5}{4},$

(g) $y = -\dfrac{5x}{4} + 5 \Rightarrow m = -\dfrac{5}{4}, c = 5$

Translations of the quadratic curve

The graph of the quadratic function $y = ax^2 + bx + c$ may be obtained from the graph of $y = x^2$ through a series of scalings and translations. The questions in this tasksheet explore the translations involved in obtaining the graph of $y = (x + p)^2 + q$ from that of $y = x^2$.

It should become apparent that the graph of $y = (x + p)^2 + q$ is a parabola with vertex at $(-p, q)$. It may be drawn by translating the graph of $y = x^2$ by $\begin{bmatrix} -p \\ q \end{bmatrix}$.

1

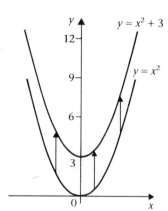

The graph of $y = x^2 + 3$ is that of $y = x^2$ translated upwards by 3 units.

2 Similarly, the graph of $y = x^2 + q$ is that of $y = x^2$ translated upwards by q units. This is not surprising since to get from $y = x^2$ to $y = x^2 + q$ you simply add q to the y-coordinates.

3

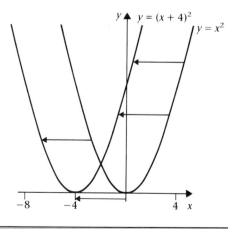

The graph of $y = (x + 4)^2$ is that of $y = x^2$ translated 4 units to the left.

4   Similarly, the graph of $y = (x + p)^2$ is that of $y = x^2$ translated p units to the left. Notice that the vertex occurs when $x = -p$, not at $x = p$.

5   To obtain the graph of $y = (x + p)^2 + q$, the graph of $y = x^2$ is translated through p units to the left and q units upwards. The vertex of the resulting parabola is at $(-p, q)$, and its line of symmetry has equation $x = -p$.

6   (a) $y = x^2 + 3$

(b) $y = (x - 2)^2$

(c) $y = x^2 - 4$

(d) $y = (x + 5)^2$

(e) $y = (x - 2)^2 + 3$

(f) $y = -x^2 + 4$

(g) $y = -(x - 3)^2$

(h) $y = -(x - 2)^2 + 4$

(i) $y = (x + 2)^2 + 5$

(j) $y = -(x - 1)^2 - 1$

(k) $y = -(x + 2)^2 + 4$

(l) $y = (x - 1)^2 - 1$

Translations of the quadratic curve

The graph of the quadratic function $y = ax^2 + bx + c$ may be obtained from the graph of $y = x^2$ through a series of scalings and translations. The questions in this tasksheet explore the translations involved in obtaining the graph of $y = (x + p)^2 + q$ from that of $y = x^2$.

It should become apparent that the graph of $y = (x + p)^2 + q$ is a parabola with vertex at

$(-p, q)$. It may be drawn by translating the graph of $y = x^2$ by $\begin{bmatrix} -p \\ q \end{bmatrix}$.

1 (a) The graph of $y = (x + p)^2 + q$ is obtained from that of $y = x^2$ by a translation of p units to the left and q units upwards.

(b) The coordinates of the vertex are $(-p, q)$.

(c) The equation of the line of symmetry is $x = -p$.

(d) The graph crosses the x-axis twice if $q < 0$, it touches the x-axis once if $q = 0$ and it does not meet the x-axis if $q > 0$.

2 (a) $y = x^2 + 3$ (b) $y = (x - 2)^2$ (c) $y = x^2 - 4$

(d) $y = (x + 5)^2$ (e) $y = (x - 2)^2 + 3$ (f) $y = -x^2 + 4$

(g) $y = -(x - 2)^2 + 4$ (h) $y = (x + 2)^2 - 4$

3 The curves meet at $(-2, 0)$ and $(2, 0)$.

4 The curves meet at $(0, 11)$ and $(6, 11)$.

5 The vertex of $y = (x + 2)^2 + 3$ is at $(-2, 3)$.   So $y = ax^2$ passes through $(-2, 3)$.

Substituting in the equation gives

$$3 = a(-2)^2$$
$$\Rightarrow 3 = 4a$$
$$\Rightarrow a = \tfrac{3}{4}$$

6 The curves must be parallel, so $a = c$ and $b \neq d$.

Multiplying brackets

1 (a) $5x + 15$ (b) $2x - 8$

   (c) $16x + 40$ (d) $-2x - 12$

   (e) $-4x + 28$ (f) $6x - 12y$

2 (a) $3 + 2x + 6 = 9 + 2x$

   (b) $3x - 12$

   (c) $a + 40 - 5a = 40 - 4a$

   (d) $t - 4 + 4t = 5t - 4$

   (e) $p - 1 + 6p - 16 = 7p - 17$

   (f) $5 - 30x + 54 = 59 - 30x$

   (g) $y - 9y + 18 = 18 - 8y$

   (h) $4x - 2x + x^2 = 2x + x^2$

   (i) $2 - 3x - 6x^2$

3 (a) $x^2 + 6x + 8$ (b) $x^2 - 2x - 3$

   (c) $x^2 + 3x - 4$ (d) $x^2 - 7x + 10$

   (e) $x^2 - 2x - 35$ (f) $x^2 + 10x + 16$

   (g) $x^2 - 11x + 18$ (h) $x^2 + 3x - 28$

4 (a)   (i) $x^2 + 6x + 9$

      (ii) $x^2 + 14x + 49$

      (iii) $x^2 - 18x + 81$

      (iv) $x^2 - 12x + 36$

   (b)   (i) $b = 2p$

      (ii) $c = p^2$

Completing the square

If you wish to sketch the graph of a quadratic function given in the conventional form $y = x^2 + bx + c$, then it is helpful to be able to rewrite it in the 'completed square' form $y = (x + p)^2 + q$, so that the translation from $y = x^2$ is obvious. This tasksheet develops an appropriate strategy.

1 (b) It can be seen from the graph that $y = x^2 + 2x$ has its vertex at $(-1, -1)$, so

a translation of $\begin{bmatrix} -1 \\ -1 \end{bmatrix}$ maps $y = x^2$ onto $y = x^2 + 2x$.

Hence $y = x^2 + 2x$ is equivalent to $y = (x + 1)^2 - 1$.

2 (ii) (a) $\begin{bmatrix} -5 \\ -25 \end{bmatrix}$ $\quad x^2 + 10x = (x + 5)^2 - 25$

(b) $\begin{bmatrix} 3 \\ -9 \end{bmatrix}$ $\quad x^2 - 6x = (x - 3)^2 - 9$

(c) $\begin{bmatrix} -3.5 \\ -12.25 \end{bmatrix}$ $\quad x^2 + 7x = (x + 3.5)^2 - 12.25$

3 (a) $x^2 + 4x = (x + 2)^2 - 4$

(b) $x^2 + 4x \qquad = (x + 2)^2 - 4$

$\Rightarrow x^2 + 4x + 9 \qquad = (x + 2)^2 - 4 + 9$

$\Rightarrow x^2 + 4x + 9 \qquad = (x + 2)^2 + 5$

4 (a) $x^2 + 14x + 2 = (x + 7)^2 - 49 + 2$

$\qquad\qquad\qquad\quad = (x + 7)^2 - 47$

(b) $x^2 - 8x + 5 \quad = (x - 4)^2 - 11$

(c) $x^2 - 3x + 1 \quad = (x - \frac{3}{2})^2 - \frac{5}{4}$

5 (a) $x^2 + bx = (x + \frac{1}{2}b)^2 - \frac{1}{4}b^2 \Rightarrow p = \frac{1}{2}b$ and $q = -\frac{1}{4}b^2$

(b) $x^2 + bx + c = (x + \frac{1}{2}b)^2 - \frac{1}{4}b^2 + c$

Halve b Subtract $\frac{1}{4}b^2$ from c

Completing the square (algebraic approach)

1 (a) (i) $x^2 + 10x + 25$ (ii) $x^2 - 6x + 9$

(b) (i) $(x + 2)^2$ (ii) $(x + 6)^2$ (iii) $(x - 5)^2$

(c) (i) $p = \frac{1}{2}b$ (ii) $c = \frac{1}{4}b^2$

2 (a) $(x + 3)^2$ (b) $(x + 3)^2 - 9$ (c) $(x + 3)^2 - 4$

(d)

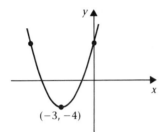

$(-3, -4)$

3 (a) (i) $(x + 6)^2 - 36$ (ii) $(x - 7)^2 - 49$

(b) (i) $(x + 6)^2 - 16$ (ii) $(x - 7)^2 + 31$

4 (a) $(x + 7)^2 - 47$ (b) $(x - \frac{3}{2})^2 - \frac{5}{4}$ (c) $(x + 4)^2 - 19$

5 (a) $(x - 1)^2$

(b) Any value squared is greater than or equal to 0. So the smallest value of $(x - 1)^2$ is 0 when $x = 1$.

6 (a) $(x + \frac{1}{2}b)^2 + c - \frac{1}{4}b^2$ (b) $(-\frac{1}{2}b, c - \frac{1}{4}b^2)$

(c) $$c - \tfrac{1}{4}b^2 > 0$$
$$\Rightarrow \quad 4c - b^2 > 0$$
$$\Rightarrow \quad 4c > b^2$$

Factorised quadratics

The completed square form of the quadratic function allows you to locate its vertex. This tasksheet attempts to show the connection between the points where the graph cuts the x-axis, the zeros of the function and the factorised form.

1 (a) The graph shows that 1 and 5 give the points $x = -1$ and $x = -5$ where the curve cuts the x-axis. The values are also the zeros of the function because

$$(x + 1)(x + 5) = 0$$
$$\Rightarrow x + 1 = 0 \text{ or } x + 5 = 0$$
$$\Rightarrow x = -1 \text{ or } x = -5$$

(b) When α and β are distinct real numbers, the graph will cross the x-axis at two points, irrespective of whether α and β are positive, negative or zero. If α and β are equal then the two crossing points coincide and the graph touches the x-axis.

(c) α and β give the points $x = -\alpha$ and $x = -\beta$ where the graph cuts the x-axis. The values $-\alpha$ and $-\beta$ are also the zeros of the function with that graph.

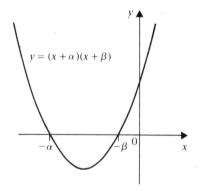

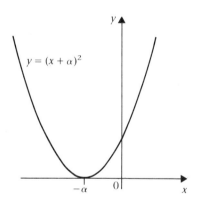

2

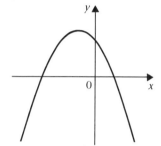

$y = -(x + \alpha)(x + \beta)$

is the reflection in
the x-axis of

$y = (x + \alpha)(x + \beta)$

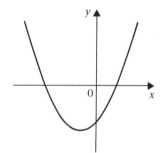

3 (a) $y = (x - 1)(x - 5)$ (b) $y = (x + 3)(x - 9)$

(c) $y = (x + 10)(x + 2)$ (d) $y = x(x - 4)$

(e) $y = -(x - 1)(x - 5)$ (f) $y = -(x + 2)(x - 6)$

(g) $y = -(x + 3)(x + \frac{1}{2})$ (h) $y = -x(x - 2)$

(i) $y = (x + 3)(x - 3)$ (j) $y = -(x - 7)^2$

(k) $y = (x + 2)^2$ (l) $y = -(x + 5)(x - 5)$

Further factorisation

This tasksheet provides a background from which a strategy for factorising $x^2 + bx + c$ can be developed. The relationship between the constant term c and the factorised form is examined and this relationship is used to help select appropriate pairs of factors.

1 (a) (i) $x^2 + 5x + 6$ (ii) $x^2 - 5x + 6$

       (iii) $x^2 + 9x + 20$ (iv) $x^2 - 9x + 20$

   (b) The constant term c is obtained by multiplying together the numbers in the brackets, together with their signs ($+$ or $-$). For example,

$$(x - 2)(x + 3) = x^2 + x - 6$$

$$-2 \ \times \ 3 = -6$$

   (c) The coefficient b is obtained by adding together the numbers in the brackets. For example,

$$(x - 2)(x + 3) = x^2 + x - 6$$

$$-2 \ + \ 3 = 1$$

2 (a) $(x + 2)(x + 7)$ (b) $(x + 8)(x + 5)$ (c) $(x - 2)(x - 7)$

    (d) $(x + 6)^2$ (e) $(x - 8)(x + 1)$ (f) $(x + 7)(x - 4)$

    (g) $(x - 6)(x - 2)$ (h) $(x - 9)(x + 4)$ (i) $(x - 8)(x + 6)$

    (j) $(x + 6)(x - 4)$

3 (a) $x(x + 2)$ (b) $(x + 3)(x - 3)$ (c) $x(x - 8)$

    (d) Not possible   (e) $x(x + 25)$ (f) $(x + 5)(x - 5)$

    (g) Not possible   (h) $(x + 1)(x - 1)$ (i) $x(x - 1)$

2 Sequences

2.2 Generating sequences

1 U is the sequence 2, 8, 14, 20, . . .

    (a) What are the values of u_1 and u_4?

    (b) What value would you expect for u_5?
Give an equation connecting u_5 and u_4.

    (c) Give an equation connecting u_{i+1} and u_i.

2 T is the sequence defined by $t_1 = 4$ and $t_{i+1} = t_i + 9$.

    (a) What are the values of t_2, t_3, t_4, t_5?

    (b) What is the value of t_{20}?

---

1 (a) u_1 is the first term, which is 2.
u_4 is the fourth term, which is 20.

  (b) Following the pattern of the sequence (each term being 6 more than the previous one) the fifth term, u_5, is obtained by adding 6 to the fourth term, u_4.

$$u_5 = 26$$
$$u_5 = u_4 + 6$$

  (c) Similarly

$$u_{i+1} = u_i + 6$$

2 (a) $t_2 = 4 + 9 = 13$

$$t_3 = 13 + 9 = 22$$

$$t_4 = 31$$

$$t_5 = 40$$

  (b) $t_{20} = 4 + (19 \times 9) = 175$

2.3 The general term

> (a) Why is $2 \times 3^{n-1}$ the general term of the sequence T where
>
> $$t_{i+1} = 3t_i \text{ and } t_1 = 2?$$
>
> (b) What are the terms of the sequence U where
>
> $$u_i = (-1)^i \frac{1}{i^2} ?$$

(a) Each term is 3 times the previous term,

so $t_2 = 2 \times 3$
$t_3 = (2 \times 3) \times 3 = 2 \times 3^2$
$t_4 = (2 \times 3 \times 3) \times 3 = 2 \times 3^3$

To obtain t_n, t_1 must be multiplied by 3 a total of $n-1$ times. Therefore, $t_n = 2 \times 3^{n-1}$.

(b) $u_1 = (-1)^1 \frac{1}{1} = -1 \qquad u_2 = (-1)^2 \frac{1}{4} = \frac{1}{4}$

$u_3 = (-1)^3 \frac{1}{9} = -\frac{1}{9} \qquad u_4 = (-1)^4 \frac{1}{16} = \frac{1}{16}$ etc.

The $(-1)^i$ causes the sign to change for alternate terms.

2.4 Arithmetic series

> As a schoolboy, the German mathematician Gauss (1777–1855) spotted a simple fact which helped him to calculate the sum of the series:
>
> $$1 + 2 + 3 + 4 + \ldots + 99 + 100$$
>
> Can you find a simple way to sum this series?

The numbers from 1 to 100 can be paired up into 50 pairs each with a total of 101 as shown:

$$1 + 2 + 3 + \ldots + 99 + 100$$

The total is therefore $50 \times 101 = 5050$.

2.5 Finance

Which scheme should Jo choose?

After one year at 8% per annum, Jo's £1000 will be worth £1080. If she invests at 4% payable every six months, her investment is worth £1040 after six months and £1040 × $\frac{104}{100}$ = £1081.60 after one year. This is equivalent to 8.16% per annum and is therefore better.

2.6 Sigma notation

(a) How much is Jo's first investment of £1000 worth after ten years?

(b) How much is Jo's second investment of £1000 worth at the end of the ten year period?

(c) Explain why her total investment is worth

£1000(1.08 + 1.08^2 + 1.08^3 + ... + 1.08^{10}) after ten years.

(a) After one year her investment is worth £1000 × 1.08,
after two years it is worth £1000 × 1.08^2,
after three years it is worth £1000 × 1.08^3,
and after ten years it is worth £1000 × 1.08^{10} = £2158.92.

(b) Since her second investment will earn interest for nine years it will be worth £1000 × 1.08^9 = £1999.00.

(c) Continuing this pattern, her third investment will be worth £1000 × 1.08^8 since it earns interest for eight years.

Her final investment earns interest for one year and will be worth £1000 × 1.08^1.

Her total investment is therefore

$$£(1000 \times 1.08^1 + 1000 \times 1.08^2 + ... + 1000 \times 1.08^{10})$$
$$= £1000 (1.08 + 1.08^2 + 1.08^3 + ... + 1.08^{10})$$

2.7 Geometric series

(a) Explain why subtracting ① from ② leads to the result

$$0.08S = 1.08^{11} - 1.08$$

(b) What is S, the amount Jo has saved after ten years?

(c) Suggest other examples of G.Ps.

(d) Generalise the method for summing the G.P. to any G.P., where the first term is a and the common ratio is r.

(a) $\begin{aligned} 1.08 \ S &= \qquad\qquad 1.08^2 + 1.08^3 + 1.08^4 + \ldots \quad + 1.08^{11} \\ S &= \quad 1.08 + 1.08^2 + 1.08^3 + \ldots \quad + 1.08^{10} \end{aligned}$

$\overline{\quad 0.08 \ S = -1.08 \qquad\qquad\qquad\qquad\qquad\qquad + 1.08^{11}}$

since all the other terms cancel.

Therefore, $0.08S = 1.08^{11} - 1.08$

(b) From (a), $S = \dfrac{1.08^{11} - 1.08}{0.08} = 15.645$

Thus, after ten years Jo has saved £15 645.

(c) Examples might include cases where

(i) the first term is not 1, for example 2, 6, 18, 54, . . .

(ii) the common ratio is less than 1, for example 2, 1, $\frac{1}{2}$, $\frac{1}{4}$ . . .

(iii) the common ratio is negative, for example 2, -1, $\frac{1}{2}$, $-\frac{1}{4}$, . . .

(d) $\qquad\qquad\begin{aligned} S &= a + ar + ar^2 + \ldots + ar^{n-1} \\ rS &= \qquad ar + ar^2 + \ldots + ar^{n-1} + ar^n \\ rS - S &= ar^n - a \\ \Rightarrow (r-1)S &= a(r^n - 1) \end{aligned}$

$\Rightarrow \qquad\qquad S = a\dfrac{(r^n - 1)}{r - 1}$

2.8 Infinity

(a) Explain what is meant by a sum to infinity.

(b) In the previous section you found that

$$\sum_{i=1}^{n} ar^{i-1} = a\,\frac{r^n - 1}{r - 1}$$

(i) For what values of r will the series have a sum to infinity?

(ii) What is this sum?

(a) For a series with an infinite number of terms, the sum to infinity is the limit of the sum to n terms as n tends to infinity.

For example, the series $1 + \dfrac{1}{2} + \dfrac{1}{4} + \dfrac{1}{8} + \ldots + \left(\dfrac{1}{2}\right)^{n-1}$ has sum

$$\frac{\left(\frac{1}{2}\right)^n - 1}{\frac{1}{2} - 1} = 2\left(1 - \left(\frac{1}{2}\right)^n\right)$$

As $n \to \infty$, the sum tends to 2.

(b) (i) If $|r| < 1$, then $r^n \to 0$ as $n \to \infty$ and so there is a sum to infinity.

(ii) The sum $\displaystyle\sum_{1}^{n} ar^{i-1} = a\left(\frac{r^n - 1}{r - 1}\right)$ therefore tends to

$$a\left(\frac{0 - 1}{r - 1}\right) = \frac{a}{1 - r}$$

Patterns and sequences

1   (a) $u_1 = -5$
Putting $i = 1$ gives $u_2 = u_1 + 2 = -5 + 2 = -3$,
putting $i = 2$ gives $u_3 = u_2 + 2 = -3 + 2 = -1$ etc.
$u_1 = -5$
$u_2 = -3$
$u_3 = -1$
$u_4 = 1$
$u_5 = 3$
$u_{20} = -5 + (19 \times 2) = 33$

   (b) $u_1 = 15$
$u_2 = 11$
$u_3 = 7$
$u_4 = 3$
$u_5 = -1$
$u_{20} = 15 - (19 \times 4) = -61$

   (c) $u_1 = 2$
$u_2 = 3 \times 2 = 6$
$u_3 = 3 \times 6 = 18$
$u_4 = 3 \times 18 = 54$
$u_5 = 3 \times 54 = 162$
$u_{20} = 3^{19} \times 2 \approx 2.3 \times 10^9$

Note how *multiplying* by 3 gives a rapid increase in magnitude.

   (d) $u_1 = 3$
$u_2 = \frac{1}{3}$
$u_3 = 3$
$u_4 = \frac{1}{3}$
$u_5 = 3$
$u_{20} = \frac{1}{3}$

The sequence oscillates.

2 (a) The sequence alternates in sign. The magnitude of each term is twice that of the previous term.
With $u_1 = 3$ for example, the sequence is $3, -6, 12, -24, 48, -96, \ldots$

   (b) The sequence diverges rapidly unless $u_1 = -4$.
If $u_1 < -4$ the sequence approaches negative infinity.
If $u_1 > -4$ the sequence approaches infinity.

   (c) If $u_1 > 0$ the sequence approaches infinity.
If $u_1 < 0$ the sequence approaches negative infinity.

   (d) The sequence approaches zero.

   (e) The sequence alternates between the values u_1 and u_2,
for example $u_1 = 7$, $u_2 = \dfrac{2}{7}$, $u_3 = 7$, $u_4 = \dfrac{2}{7}, \ldots$

   (f) The sequence increases. The difference between successive terms increases by 2 each time.

3 (a) (i) $u_1 = 1$, $u_2 = \dfrac{1}{2}$, $u_3 = \dfrac{1}{6}$, $u_4 = \dfrac{1}{24}$, $u_5 = \dfrac{1}{120}$, $u_{10} = \dfrac{1}{3\,628\,800}$

   (b) (ii) hence 10 terms are needed.

   (ii) 14 terms, $u_{14} = \dfrac{1}{87\,178\,291\,200}$

   (b) Most calculators can give $u_{69} = 1.711 \times 10^{98}$ but not u_{70}, when the exponent is greater than 99.

4E (a) If $u_1 = u_2 = 1$ the Fibonacci sequence $1, 1, 2, 3, 5, 8, 13, \ldots$ is obtained.
Otherwise, a similar sequence where each term is the sum of the two preceeding terms is obtained.

   (b) The sequence eventually converges to a value of -4 unless $u_1 = 2.5$.

   (c) If u_1 is a positive integer, the sequence eventually settles into the cycle $2, 4, 8, 6, 2, 4, \ldots$ or becomes a sequence of zeros.

5E The sequence always appears to settle into the cycle $4, 2, 1, 4, 2, 1, \ldots$ This has never been proved and is known as Thwaite's conjecture.

The general term

This tasksheet illustrates a technique that is useful when generalising results which form a pattern.

> Write down the early numbers in the pattern and, once you have a feel for what is happening, try to write down some of the later numbers in the pattern. It is then easy to write the ith term in terms of i.

1

No. of triangles	1	2	3	4	5	10	20	100	i
No. of matchsticks	3	5	7	9	11	21	41	201	$2i + 1$

In this case the idea of adding on two matches each time helps you to find the first few terms of the sequence. In order to find the later terms you need to spot that the number of matches is found by doubling the number of triangles and adding 1.

2

Position in pattern	1	2	3	4	5	10	20	100	i
No. of dots (a)	1	4	7	10	13	28	58	298	$3i - 2$
(b)	4	8	12	16	20	40	80	400	$4i$
(c)	1	3	5	7	9	19	39	199	$2i - 1$
(d)	1	4	9	16	25	100	400	10 000	i^2
(e)	2	8	18	32	50	200	800	20 000	$2i^2$
(f)	3	8	15	24	35	120	440	10 200	$i(i + 2)$

3 (a) $i = 1: u_1 = 3 \times 1 + 2 = 5$
$i = 2: u_2 = 3 \times 2 + 2 = 8$
$u_3 = 3 \times 3 + 2 = 11, u_4 = 3 \times 4 + 2 = 14, u_5 = 3 \times 5 + 2 = 17$

(b) $u_1 = 5 \times 2^1 = 10, u_2 = 5 \times 2^2 = 20, u_3 = 5 \times 2^3 = 40, u_4 = 80, u_5 = 160$

(c) $u_1 = 3 \times 1^2 = 3, u_2 = 3 \times 2^2 = 12, u_3 = 27, u_4 = 48, u_5 = 75$

4 This illustrates a useful device for writing the general term of a sequence which has alternating signs.

(a) (i) $-1, 1, -1, 1, -1, \ldots$

(ii) $1, -1, 1, -1, 1, \ldots$

(iii) $-1, 1, -1, 1, -1, \ldots$

(iv) $-1, 2, -4, 8, -16, \ldots$

(b) (i) $u_i = 3 \times (-1)^{i+1}$ (ii) $u_i = 3 \times (-1)^i$

5

	\multicolumn{5}{c}{Terms}
	5	6	9	100	i
A	10	12	18	200	$2i$
B	14	17	26	299	$3i - 1$
C	32	64	512	2^{100}	2^i
D	96	192	1536	3×2^{100}	3×2^i
E	1	-1	1	-1	$(-1)^{i+1}$
F	-5	6	-9	100	$(-1)^i i$
G	5	-6	9	-100	$(-1)^{i+1} i$
H	10	-12	18	-200	$(-1)^{i+1} 2i$
I	$\dfrac{1}{6}$	$\dfrac{1}{7}$	$\dfrac{1}{10}$	$\dfrac{1}{101}$	$\dfrac{1}{i+1}$
J	25	-36	81	$-10\,000$	$(-1)^{i+1} i^2$

Arithmetic series

1 (a) (i) Each pair of terms adds up to 21, so the total is $10 \times 21 = 210$.

    (ii) Note that, because there is an odd number of terms, not all terms pair up. However, the same result may be obtained by finding the average of the first and last terms and multiplying by the number of terms.

    The average of the first and last terms is

$$\frac{(1 + 9)}{2} = 5$$

    So the total is $9 \times 5 = 45$

    (iii) $\dfrac{(1 + 29)}{2} \times 29 = 435$

  (b) There are many possible ways. One way is to find the average of the first and last terms and multiply by the number of terms. This works for series with either an even or an odd number of terms.

2 There are many ways of doing this. For example, subtracting 4 from each term gives $1, 2, \ldots, 101$ with 101 terms.

3 (a) 50, 1275   (b) 81, 4050   (c) 101, 15150

4 The same principle applies here as in question 1. You can find the average of the first and last terms and then multiply by the number of terms.

  (a) $\dfrac{16}{2} \times 8 = 64$

  (b) $\dfrac{104}{2} \times 33 = 1716$

  (c) $\dfrac{267}{2} \times 26 = 3471$

5 (a) $1 + 2i$

  (b) $2 + 4i$

  (c) $17 - 5i$

6 (a) (i) $5 + (4 \times 14) = 61$ (ii) $\dfrac{5 + 61}{2} \times 15 = 495$

(b) (i) $5 + (4 \times (i - 1)) = 4i + 1$ (ii) $\dfrac{5 + 4i + 1}{2} \times i = i(2i + 3)$

7 (a) $a + 4d$ (b) $a + 49d$

(c) $a + (n - 1)d$ (d) $\dfrac{a + (a + 49d)}{2} \times 50 = 25(2a + 49d)$

9 (a) $a = 2, d = 5, n = 20;$ $S = 10 \times (4 + (19 \times 5)) = 990$

(b) $a = 19, d = -3, n = 50;$ $S = 25 \times (38 - (49 \times 3)) = -2725$

10 (a) $2n - 1$

(b) 7 (This uses 49 bricks.)

(c) $S = \frac{1}{2}n (2 + (n-1)2)$

$= \frac{1}{2}n (2n)$

$= n^2$

11E (a) $4n - 2$

(b) $S = \frac{1}{2}n (4 + (n-1)4)$
$= 2n^2$

This is twice as many as in question 10.

12E (a) $£(5 + 10 + \ldots + 90) = £855.$

(b) $\frac{5}{2}n(n + 1) \ > 500$

$\Rightarrow n(n + 1) > 200$

$\Rightarrow n = 14$

13E $8.2 + 8.3 + \ldots = 22\,000$

$\frac{1}{2}n (16.4 + (n-1) \times 0.1) = 22\,000$

$n(n + 163) = 440\,000$

$n \approx 587$

Annual percentage rate

1 £1200 is repaid, which includes £400 interest. This is a rate of 50%.

2 The outstanding debt after 12 months is £0 (approximately!) and so the debt is fully repaid.

3 £100 × 1.0165^{12} = £121.699.
The original £100 must be repaid together with interest of approximately 21.7%.

4 (a) 12.7%   (b) 26.8%   (c) 79.6%

5 Possibly the simplest algorithm is:
divide rate by 100,
add 1,
raise to the power 12,
subtract 1,
multiply by 100.

6 The reversed algorithm is:
divide APR by 100,
add 1,
find the 12th root,
subtract 1,
multiply by 100.

The rate is 5.95%.

8 7.93% (7.93083%), 149.9%.

9 (a) $\frac{30}{100}$ × 7292.86

(b) 2187.86 + 36 × 127.52 + 1786.75

(c) 12 months and 52 weeks are assumed to be equivalent with

29.43 = $\frac{12}{52}$ × 127.52

(d) 0.9788745% (approximately!)

For normally-structured financial facilities, companies have printed charts for APR. More unusually structured facilities like that for the Citroen BX 16RE are often calculated using special financial calculators, with functions embodying the approved methods of calculating APR. The regulations and financial formulas relating to APR calculation are governed by the Consumer Credit Act 1974 and form a very detailed body of information with prescribed mathematical techniques.

Mortgages

1 Year one:

		£
Initial loan		40 000
Interest		4 000
Total debt		44 000
Repayments 12 at £395		4 740
Outstanding balance		39 260

Year two:

		£
Loan outstanding		39 260
Interest		3 926
Total debt		43 186
Repayments 12 at £395		4 740
Outstanding balance		38 446

2 (a) $L_1 = 40000$

(b) $L_{n+1} = L_n \times 1.1 - 4740$

3 L_{20} is negative and so the mortgage will be paid off during its 20th year.

Using sigma

1 (a) $\displaystyle\sum_1^n u_i$

(b) The sum is multiplied by the constant.

(c) $\displaystyle\sum_1^n au_i = au_1 + \ldots + au_n$

$\qquad = a(u_1 + \ldots + u_n)$

$\qquad = a\displaystyle\sum_1^n u_i$

2 (a) The sum is increased by n times the constant.

(b) $\displaystyle\sum_1^n (u_i + b) = u_1 + b + u_2 + b + \ldots + u_n + b$

$\qquad = u_1 + \ldots + u_n + nb$

$\qquad = \displaystyle\sum_1^n u_i + nb$

(c) $\displaystyle\sum_1^n (au_i + b) = \sum_1^n au_i + nb$

$\qquad = a\displaystyle\sum_1^n u_i + nb$

3 (a) $2\displaystyle\sum_1^n i - 3n \quad = n(n+1) - 3n$

$\qquad = n^2 - 2n$

(b) $5\displaystyle\sum_1^n i + n \quad = \dfrac{5}{2}n(n+1) + n$

$\qquad = \dfrac{5}{2}n^2 + \dfrac{7}{2}n$

4 $\displaystyle\sum_1^n (u_i + v_i) \quad = u_1 + v_1 + u_2 + v_2 + \ldots + u_n + v_n$

$\qquad = (u_1 + u_2 + \ldots + u_n) + (v_1 + v_2 + \ldots + v_n)$

$\qquad = \displaystyle\sum_1^n u_i + \sum_1^n v_i$

5 (a) $(n + 1)^3 - 1^3$. The other terms cancel out in pairs.

(b) This is part (a) written in Σ notation.

(c) $(i + 1)^3 - i^3 = 3i^2 + 3i + 1$

$$\sum_1^n (i + 1)^3 - \sum_1^n i^3 = \sum_1^n \left[(i + 1)^3 - i^3 \right]$$

$$= \sum_1^n (3i^2 + 3i + 1)$$

$$= 3 \sum_1^n i^2 + 3 \sum_1^n i + n$$

(d) $3 \sum_1^n i^2 + 3 \sum_1^n i + n = (n + 1)^3 - 1$

$$3 \sum_1^n i^2 + \frac{3n(n + 1)}{2} + n = n^3 + 3n^2 + 3n$$

$$3 \sum_1^n i^2 = n^3 + \frac{3n^2}{2} + \frac{n}{2}$$

$$\sum_1^n i^2 = \frac{(2n^3 + 3n^2 + n)}{6}$$

$$\sum_1^n i^2 = \frac{n(n + 1)(2n + 1)}{6}$$

6 $\dfrac{99 \times 100 \times 199}{6} = 328\,350$

7 (a) $2\sum_{1}^{n} i^2 - 6\sum_{1}^{n} i + 4n = \dfrac{n(n+1)(2n+1)}{3} - 3n(n+1) + 4n$

$\qquad\qquad\qquad = \dfrac{n(2n^2 - 6n + 4)}{3}$

$\qquad\qquad\qquad = \dfrac{2n(n-1)(n-2)}{3}$

(b) $\sum_{1}^{n} (2i-1)^2 = \sum_{1}^{n} (4i^2 - 4i + 1)$

$\qquad\qquad\quad = 4\sum_{1}^{n} i^2 - 4\sum_{1}^{n} i + n$

$\qquad\qquad\quad = \dfrac{2n(n+1)(2n+1)}{3} - 2n(n+1) + n$

$\qquad\qquad\quad = \dfrac{n(4n^2 - 1)}{3}$

$\qquad\qquad\quad = \dfrac{n(2n-1)(2n+1)}{3}$

Mortgages revisited

1 After 3 years, final debt $= \{40\,000 \times 1.1^2 - 4740\,(1.1 + 1)\} \times 1.1 - 4740$
$= 40\,000 \times 1.1^3 - 4740\,(1.1^2 + 1.1 + 1)$

After 4 years, final debt $= \{40\,000 \times 1.1^3 - 4740\,(1.1^2 + 1.1 + 1)\} \times 1.1 - 4740$
$= 40\,000 \times 1.1^4 - 4740\,(1.1^3 + 1.1^2 + 1.1 + 1)$

2 (a) $\displaystyle\sum_{i=1}^{n} 1.1^{i-1}$ is a G.P. with first term 1 and common ratio 1.1.

The sum of n terms of this G.P. is $\quad 1 \times \dfrac{1.1^n - 1}{1.1 - 1} = \dfrac{1.1^n - 1}{0.1}$

(b) $40\,000 \times 1.1^n - 4740 \displaystyle\sum_{i=1}^{n} 1.1^{i-1} = 40\,000 \times 1.1^n - 47\,40 \times \dfrac{1.1^n - 1}{0.1}$

$= 40\,000 \times 1.1^n - 47\,400 \times (1.1^n - 1)$

$= 40\,000 \times 1.1^n - 47\,400 \times 1.1^n + 47\,400$

$= 47\,400 - 7400 \times 1.1^n$

3 Let £P be the monthly payment.

After 1 year,   final debt $= 50\,000 \times 1.11 - 12P$
After 2 years,   final debt $= 50\,000 \times 1.11^2 - 12P\,(1.11 + 1)$
After 3 years,   final debt $= 50\,000 \times 1.11^3 - 12P\,(1.11^2 + 1.11 + 1)$
After 25 years, final debt $= 50\,000 \times 1.11^{25} - 12P\,(1.11^{24} + \ldots + 1.11 + 1)$

$= 50\,000 \times 1.11^{25} - 12P \displaystyle\sum_{i=1}^{25} 1.1^{i-1}$

$= 50\,000 \times 1.11^{25} - 12P \left(\dfrac{1.11^{25} - 1}{0.11} \right)$

Since the debt is reduced to zero,

$\Rightarrow 50\,000 \times 1.11^{25} - 12P \left(\dfrac{1.11^{25} - 1}{0.11} \right) = 0$

$\Rightarrow \qquad\qquad\qquad 50\,000 \times 1.11^{25} = 12P \left(\dfrac{1.11^{25} - 1}{0.11} \right)$

$\Rightarrow \qquad\qquad\qquad 679\,273.19 = 1372.9597P$

$\Rightarrow \qquad\qquad\qquad 494.751\,00 = P$

In practice, a monthly repayment of £494.76 would be required.

Zeno's Paradox

1   (a) Since the rabbit is running at half the speed of the dog, the rabbit will have run 64 m.

   (b) By the same argument, the rabbit will have run a further 32 m.

   (c) 16 m.

The argument appears to suggest that the dog will never catch the rabbit because the dog always has to reach the spot last occupied by the rabbit. In the meantime the rabbit will have moved on ahead again. However, you know that, in practice, the dog will catch the rabbit!

2   This is a G.P, first term 128, common ratio $\dfrac{1}{2}$

   (a) $D = \dfrac{128\left(1 - (\frac{1}{2})^n\right)}{1 - \frac{1}{2}} = 256\left(1 - \left(\dfrac{1}{2}\right)^n\right)$ m

   (b) As n approaches infinity, $(\frac{1}{2})^n \to 0$ and so $D \to 256$.

3   This is a G.P., first term 64, common ratio $\frac{1}{2}$.

   (a) $R = 64 \times \dfrac{1 - (\frac{1}{2})^n}{1 - (\frac{1}{2})} = 128\left(1 - \left(\dfrac{1}{2}\right)^n\right)$

   (b) As n approaches infinity, $\left(\dfrac{1}{2}\right)^n \to 0$ and so $R \to 128$.

4   (a) $40 \times 8 = 320$ m

   (b) $40 \times 4 = 160$ m

   (c) Since the dog will have run 160 m further than the rabbit it will have caught up with it.

5 The answer to question 2 suggests that the dog will never travel more than 256 m. You know this must be false! The paradox is resolved when you realise that *time* must be taken into account. The distances in question 2 are taken over decreasing periods of time and so give a false impression of the motion.

The dog runs 128 m in 16 seconds, the next 64 m in 8 seconds, the next 32 m in 4 seconds etc. The total time is therefore

$$16 + 8 + 4 + 2 + \ldots = \frac{16}{1 - \frac{1}{2}} = 32 \text{ seconds.}$$

In 32 seconds the dog will have run 256 m, as predicted. However, the dog does not stop moving after 32 seconds and will now overtake the rabbit who has run $4 \times 32 = 128$ m and is level at this point.

3 Functions and graphs

3.1 Function notation

Compare the notations

$$f(c) = \frac{20}{2^c} \text{ and } L = \frac{20}{2^c}.$$

What are the advantages and disadvantages of each notation?

The notation $L = \dfrac{20}{2^c}$ shows very simply the relationship between

two variables where one variable is dependent upon the other.

$f(c) = \dfrac{20}{2^c}$ emphasises that the quantity $\dfrac{20}{2^c}$ is dependent upon c,

and provides a convenient notation for referring to particular values: $f(0), f(1)$ etc.

3.2 Using function notation

(a) Write down y in completed square form.

(b) What is $f(x + 3) - 4$?

(a) $y = x^2 + 6x + 5$
   $\Rightarrow y = (x + 3)^2 - 4$

(b) $f(x) = x^2$
   $\Rightarrow$ $f(x + 3) = (x + 3)^2$
   $\Rightarrow$ $f(x + 3) - 4 = (x + 3)^2 - 4$
                  $= x^2 + 6x + 5$

3.3 Defining functions

Why would it be meaningless to calculate f(-2) or f(1 000 000)?

It is impossible to have a negative concentration, or a concentration of 1 000 000 mg per cm³, which is the same as 1 kg per cm³. These values lie outside the **domain** of the function.

3.4 To plot or to sketch?

(a) What do you think the graph of $y = 4x + \dfrac{1}{2x - 5}$ looks like?

(b) What are the values of y when $x = 2.45, 2.49, 2.499$?

(c) What happens when $x = 2.5$?

(d) Use the graph plotter to draw the graph for values of x from 0 to 5.

Did you expect the graph to look like this?

(a) There is a temptation here just to join up the crosses with a smooth curve.

(b) $y = -0.2, y = -40.04, y = -490.004$.

These values show that y decreases very rapidly as x approaches 2.5 from below.

(c) When $x = 2.5$, $2x - 5 = 0$ and $\dfrac{1}{2x - 5}$ is not defined.

At this point there is a discontinuity in the graph.

(d) The graph plotter shows the discontinuity at $x = 2.5$.

Important features of the graph can be missed if you simply plot points. It is therefore necessary to be able to recognise these features of a graph from its equation.

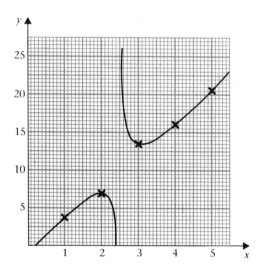

3.5 Features of graphs

> What further information do you need in order to establish which is the correct form?

1   The three graphs have different numbers of intersections with the x-axis. In order to establish the correct form you could therefore find the zeros of the function by factorising the cubic.

2   Alternatively, you could try to find the position of the minimum points. A method of doing this is given in the unit *Introductory calculus*.

3   It is easy to study the function using a graph plotter and so it is not usually worth factorising or using calculus simply to sketch the graph.

Translations

1 (b) $f(x - 2) + 5 = (x - 2)^2 + 5 = x^2 - 4x + 4 + 5 = x^2 - 4x + 9$

(c)

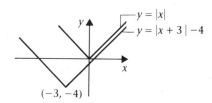

$f(x) = x^2$ $f(x) = x^2 - 4x + 9$

$(2, 5)$

The graph of $f(x - 2) + 5$ is obtained from the graph of $f(x)$ by a translation of $\begin{bmatrix} 2 \\ 5 \end{bmatrix}$.

2 (a) (ii) $g(x - 2) + 5 = (x - 2)^3 + 5 = x^3 - 6x^2 + 12x - 3$

(b) (ii) $g(x - 2) + 5 = 2^{x-2} + 5$

(c) (ii) $g(x - 2) + 5 = \sqrt{x - 2} + 5$

     (iii) In each case, a translation of $\begin{bmatrix} 2 \\ 5 \end{bmatrix}$ will superimpose $g(x)$ onto $g(x - 2) + 5$.

3

$y = |x|$

$y = |x + 3| - 4$

$(-3, -4)$

4 The graph of $f(x)$ is translated onto the graph of $f(x + a) + b$ by a translation of $\begin{bmatrix} -a \\ b \end{bmatrix}$, for any function f.

5E The effect of a is to translate the graph through $-a$ parallel to the x-axis.

The effect of b is to translate the graph through b parallel to the y-axis.

The graph of $\sin(x + a) + b$ will be identical to the graph of $\sin x$ if $b = 0$ and a is any multiple of 2π.

6E The effect of a is a stretch, parallel to the y-axis.

The effect of b is a stretch, parallel to the x-axis.

The effect of c is a translation, parallel to the x-axis.

The effect of d is a translation, parallel to the y-axis.

Dominance

1 (b) All the graphs pass through (0, 0) and (1, 1).

   (c) $y = x^5$ increases most rapidly and $y = x^2$ least rapidly. The graphs for the higher powers of x become steeper more rapidly than those for the lower powers of x as x increases above 1 or decreases below -1.

   (d) The graphs of the even powers of x have line symmetry in the y-axis, and the graphs of odd powers have rotational symmetry of order 2 about the origin.

2 (b) When x is a large positive or negative number the graphs of $y = x^2$ and $y = x^2 + 4x$ are **similar**, in that, although they are not very close to each other, they increase at a similar rate. The x^2 term is said to be **dominant**.

   (c) When x is a small positive or negative number the graphs of $y = 4x$ and $y = x^2 + 4x$ are very close together; the x^2 term has very little effect and the $4x$ term is said to be **dominant**.

The ideas in question 2 are amplified in questions 3 and 4.

> For the graph of a polynomial function, the terms of smallest degree are dominant when x is a small positive or negative number, and those of highest degree are dominant when x is a large positive or negative number.

3 The graph of $y = x^3 - 4x^2$ is similar to that of $y = -4x^2$ for small values of x and is similar to that of $y = x^3$ for large values of x.

4 The graph of $y = x^3 + x^2 - 2x + 1$ is similar to that of $y = -2x + 1$ for small values of x and is similar to that of $y = x^3$ for large values of x.

5 The graph crosses the x-axis at $x = 0, -1$ and 3. These values are related to the factors of $3x + 2x^2 - x^3$, i.e. x, $(x + 1)$ and $(3 - x)$. They are the solutions of $x = 0$, $x + 1 = 0$ and $3 - x = 0$.

In the expansion of $x(x + 1)(3 - x)$ the term of highest degree is $-x^3$ and the term of lowest degree is $3x$: so the graph of $y = x(x + 1)(3 - x)$ is similar to the graph of $y = -x^3$ for large positive and negative values of x, and to the graph of $y = 3x$ for small positive and negative values of x near the origin.

6 (a) $-x^3$ (b) x^2

   (c) $2x^2 - x^3$ (You might have thought of trying $x^2 - x^3$ first.)

4 Expressions and equations

4.1 The language of algebra

(a) Suppose that an A4 sheet has width 1 unit and length l units. What are the dimensions of an A5 sheet?

(b) Determine the value of l and check your result with the actual dimensions of A4 and A5 paper.

(c) The A0 size has an area $1\,m^2$. What is the area of the A4 size? Verify your answer by measurement.

(a) The A5 sheet has length 1 and width $\frac{1}{2}l$.

(b)

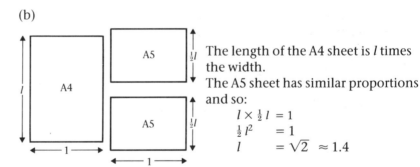

The length of the A4 sheet is l times the width.
The A5 sheet has similar proportions and so:

$$l \times \tfrac{1}{2}l = 1$$
$$\tfrac{1}{2}l^2 = 1$$
$$l = \sqrt{2} \approx 1.4$$

The measured width of A4 paper should be between 21.0 cm and 21.1 cm and the measured length between 29.7 cm and 29.8 cm.

The measured width of A5 paper should be between 14.8 cm and 14.9 cm and the measured length between 20.9 cm and 21.1 cm.

Thus the ratio of length to width is approximately 1.41 in each case.

(c)

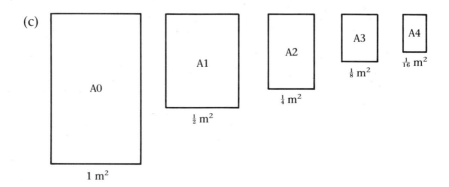

$$\text{Area of A4} = \tfrac{1}{16} \times (\text{Area of A0}) = \tfrac{1}{16} \times (100 \times 100)\,\text{cm}^2$$
$$= 625\,\text{cm}^2$$

4.2 Quadratic equations

> Express $x^2 - 4x - 4$ in completed square form. Hence solve
> $x^2 - 4x - 4 = 0$.

$$x^2 - 4x = (x-2)^2 - 4$$
$$\Rightarrow x^2 - 4x - 4 = (x-2)^2 - 8$$

$$x^2 - 4x - 4 = 0$$
$$\Rightarrow (x-2)^2 - 8 = 0$$
$$\Rightarrow (x-2)^2 = 8$$
$$\Rightarrow x - 2 = \pm \sqrt{8}$$
$$\Rightarrow x = 2 \pm \sqrt{8}$$
$$\Rightarrow x = 4.83 \text{ taking the positive root of the equation.}$$

4.3 Inequalities

> (a) Find the solution set for the following inequalities:
>
> (i) $(x + 1)(x - 2) > 0$;
>
> (ii) $(x + 1)(x - 2) > 4$.
>
> (b) Find the first triangular number greater than 100.

(a) (i) From the graph you can see that

$$x > 2 \text{ or } x < -1$$

(ii) The graph of $y = (x + 1)(x - 2)$ crosses $y = 4$ at $x = -2$ and $x = 3$. So

$$x > 3 \text{ or } x < -2$$

(b) You need to solve $\dfrac{n(n + 1)}{2} > 100$

i.e. $n^2 + n - 200 > 0$.

It can be seen that the graph cuts the x-axis between 13 and 14. The first triangular number greater than 100 is therefore the 14th.

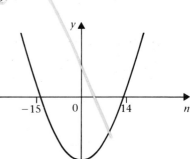

4.4 Polynomials

> How are the zeros of P(x) related to the factors?

The zeros of P(x) can be found by determining the values of x which make the **factors** zero.

$$P(x) = (x + 1)(x - 2)(x + 4)$$

The value $x = -1$ makes the first factor zero and so -1 is a root. The other roots are $+2$ and -4.

Solving problems

1 (a) The sum of 3 consecutive numbers is always 3 times the middle number.

(b) $n + (n + 1) + (n + 2) = 3n + 3 = 3(n + 1)$, giving the sum as 3 times the middle number $(n + 1)$ as expected.

2 (a) For example $9^2 - 7^2 = 81 - 49 = 32 = 4 \times 8$.

(b) Any 2 consecutive odd numbers can be written algebraically as $2n - 1, 2n + 1$. The difference between their squares is given by

$$(2n + 1)^2 - (2n - 1)^2 = 4n^2 + 4n + 1 - (4n^2 - 4n + 1)$$
$$= 4n^2 + 4n + 1 - 4n^2 + 4n - 1$$
$$= 8n$$

which is a multiple of 8.

3 The problem can be represented by the diagram

By Pythagoras,

$$(18 - h)^2 = h^2 + 6^2$$
$$324 - 36h + h^2 = h^2 + 36$$
$$36h = 288$$
$$h = 8.$$

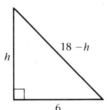

The bamboo is divided into pieces of lengths 8 and 10 cubits.

4 Treating the area as one large square, it is $(a + b)^2$.

Treating the area as one small square (area c^2) and four triangles (each of area $\frac{1}{2} ab$), it is $c^2 + 4 \times \frac{1}{2} ab = c^2 + 2ab$.

Equating these two expressions for the area gives

$$(a + b)^2 = c^2 + 2ab$$
$$\Rightarrow \quad a^2 + b^2 + 2ab = c^2 + 2ab$$
$$\Rightarrow \quad a^2 + b^2 = c^2$$

Since a, b and c are the three sides of each of the right-angled triangles in the diagram, this proves Pythagoras' theorem.

Review of equations

1 (a) $x = -6$

(b) $x = -\frac{3}{2}$

(c) $x = -\frac{9}{2}$

(d) $x = -6$

(e) $x = -3$

(f) $x = -\frac{1}{3}$

2 (a) $x = 3$ or -5

(b) $x = 0$ or 2

(c) $x = 3$ or -6

(d) $x = -2$ or 5

(e) $x = 0$ or 4

(f) $x = 3$

3 (a) $x = -7$ or 7

(b) $x = -3$ or 3

(c) $x = -3$ or 3

(d) $x = -7$ or 5

(e) $x = 0$ or 5

(f) $x = -1$ or 1

Quadratic equations

1 $x^2 + 6x + 4 = 0$ $\Rightarrow$ $(x + 3)^2 - 5 = 0$

$\Rightarrow$ $x + 3 = -\sqrt{5}$ or $\sqrt{5}$

$\Rightarrow$ $x \approx -5.24$ or -0.76

2 (a) $x^2 + bx + \dfrac{b^2}{4} = \left(x + \dfrac{b}{2}\right)^2$

$\Rightarrow x^2 + bx = \left(x + \dfrac{b}{2}\right)^2 - \dfrac{b^2}{4}$

(b) $-c = -\dfrac{4c}{4}$

(c) The squares of both $\pm \dfrac{\sqrt{b^2 - 4c}}{2}$ are equal to $\dfrac{b^2 - 4c}{4}$.

3 (a) $x = \dfrac{-6 \pm \sqrt{6^2 - 16}}{2} \approx -5.24$ or -0.76

(b) $x = \dfrac{6 \pm \sqrt{6^2 - 16}}{2} \approx 0.76$ or 5.24

(c) $x^2 + 3x - 5 = 0$

$x = \dfrac{-3 \pm \sqrt{3^2 + 20}}{2} \approx -4.19$ or 1.19

4 (a) $a = 1, b = -4, c = -4$

$x = \dfrac{4 \pm \sqrt{16 + 16}}{2}$

$x \approx -0.83$ or 4.83

(b) $a = 3, b = -7, c = -2$

$x = \dfrac{7 \pm \sqrt{49 + 24}}{6}$

$x \approx -0.26$ or 2.59

(c) $a = 3, b = -4, c = -1$

$x = \dfrac{4 \pm \sqrt{16 + 12}}{6}$

$x \approx -0.22$ or 1.55

5E There is a number of good methods you could use.

(1)
$$ax^2 + bx + c = 0$$
$$\Rightarrow \quad 4a^2x^2 + 4abx + 4ac = 0 \qquad \text{Multiply by } 4a.$$
$$\Rightarrow \quad (2ax + b)^2 - b^2 + 4ac = 0 \qquad \text{Complete the square.}$$
$$\Rightarrow \quad (2ax + b)^2 = b^2 - 4ac$$
$$\Rightarrow \quad 2ax + b = \pm \sqrt{b^2 - 4ac}$$
$$\Rightarrow \quad x = \frac{-b \pm \sqrt{b^2 - 4ac}}{2a}$$

(2)
$$ax^2 + bx + c = 0$$
$$\Rightarrow \quad x^2 + \frac{b}{a}x + \frac{c}{a} = 0 \qquad \text{Divide by } a.$$

$$\Rightarrow \quad x = \frac{-\frac{b}{a} \pm \sqrt{\left(\frac{b}{a}\right)^2 - 4\left(\frac{c}{a}\right)}}{2} \qquad \text{Formula.}$$

$$\Rightarrow \quad x = \frac{-b \pm \sqrt{b^2 - 4ac}}{2a} \qquad \begin{array}{l} \text{Multiply top and} \\ \text{bottom by } a. \end{array}$$

(3)
$$ax^2 + bx + c = 0$$
$$\Rightarrow \quad (ax)^2 + b(ax) + ac = 0 \qquad \text{Multiply by } a.$$
$$\Rightarrow \quad ax = \frac{-b \pm \sqrt{b^2 - 4(ac)}}{2} \qquad \text{Formula.}$$
$$\Rightarrow \quad x = \frac{-b \pm \sqrt{b^2 - 4ac}}{2a} \qquad \text{Divide by } a.$$

Regular pentagons and the Fibonacci sequence

1

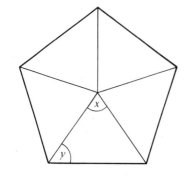

$$x = 360° \div 5 = 72°$$

$$\Rightarrow y = \frac{180° - 72°}{2} = 54° \text{ (isosceles triangle)}$$

$$\Rightarrow \text{interior angle} = 2y = 108°$$

2 $\angle$ ABC = 108° (interior angle)
Since triangle ABC is isosceles,

$$\angle \text{ BCA} = \angle \text{ BAC} = \frac{180° - 108°}{2} = 36°$$

3 BC = CD (triangle BCD isosceles).
$\Rightarrow$ CD = 1

CA = CD + DA $\Rightarrow$ DA = ϕ − 1
But $\phi \times$ DA = CD
$\Rightarrow \phi(\phi - 1) = 1$.

4 $\phi^2 - \phi - 1 = 0$ becomes

$$\left(\phi - \frac{1}{2}\right)^2 - \frac{5}{4} = 0 \quad \text{in completed square form.}$$

$$\Rightarrow \left(\phi - \frac{1}{2}\right)^2 = \frac{5}{4}$$

$$\Rightarrow \left(\phi - \frac{1}{2}\right) = \pm\sqrt{\frac{5}{4}} = \pm\frac{1}{2}\sqrt{5}$$

$$\Rightarrow \phi = \pm\frac{\sqrt{5}}{2} + \frac{1}{2} = \frac{1 \pm \sqrt{5}}{2}$$

$$\Rightarrow \phi = 1.618 \text{ or } \phi = -0.618 \text{ (to 3 decimal places)}$$

5

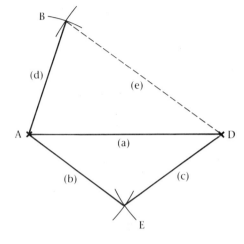

(a) Draw and measure a line segment AD = 8.1 cm. This is 5ϕ to the nearest 0.1 cm.

(b) Use compasses to draw an arc with a radius of 5 cm and centre at A.

(c) Use compasses to draw an arc with a radius of 5 cm and centre at D.

Join the point of intersection of the arcs at E to A and D, to give two sides, AE and DE, of the pentagon.

(d) Use compasses to draw an arc with a radius of 5 cm and centre at A.

(e) Use compasses to draw an arc with a radius of 8.1 cm and centre at D.

Join the point of intersection of the arcs at B to A, to give the side AB of the pentagon.

Two 5 cm arcs with their centres at B and D will give the position of C and hence the other two sides of the pentagon.

6

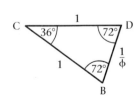

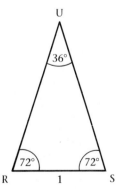

RUS is an enlargement of BCD, scale factor ϕ, hence SU = ϕ.

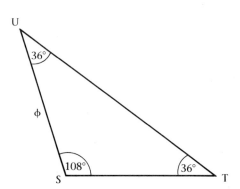

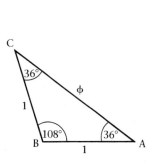

SUT is an enlargement of BCA, scale factor ϕ; hence UT $= \phi^2$

7 UT is the edge of the new pentagon.

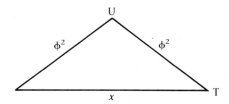

The new pentagon is an enlargement of the original pentagon, scale factor ϕ^2, hence

$$x = \phi^2 \times \phi = \phi^3.$$

8 $\phi^7 = \dfrac{1}{2}(29 + 13\sqrt{5})$; $\phi^8 = \dfrac{1}{2}(47 + 21\sqrt{5})$.

9 $\phi^7 = \dfrac{1}{2}(29 + 13\sqrt{5})$; $\psi^7 = \dfrac{1}{2}(29 - 13\sqrt{5})$.

$$\phi^7 + \psi^7 = \dfrac{1}{2}(29 + 13\sqrt{5}) + \dfrac{1}{2}(29 - 13\sqrt{5})$$

$$= \dfrac{1}{2}(29 + 29 + 13\sqrt{5} - 13\sqrt{5}) = 29$$

$$\dfrac{1}{\sqrt{5}}(\phi^7 - \psi^7) = \dfrac{1}{\sqrt{5}}\left[\dfrac{1}{2}(29 + 13\sqrt{5}) - \dfrac{1}{2}(29 - 13\sqrt{5})\right]$$

$$= \dfrac{1}{\sqrt{5}}\left[\dfrac{1}{2}(29 + 13\sqrt{5} - 29 + 13\sqrt{5})\right] = 13$$

$$\phi^8 = \frac{1}{2}(47 + 21\sqrt{5}); \qquad \psi^8 = \frac{1}{2}(47 - 21\sqrt{5})$$

$$\phi^8 + \psi^8 = \frac{1}{2}(47 + 21\sqrt{5}) + \frac{1}{2}(47 - 21\sqrt{5})$$

$$= \frac{1}{2}(47 + 47 + 21\sqrt{5} - 21\sqrt{5})$$

$$= 47$$

$$\frac{1}{\sqrt{5}}(\phi^8 - \psi^8) = \frac{1}{\sqrt{5}}\left[\frac{1}{2}(47 + 21\sqrt{5}) - \frac{1}{2}(47 - 21\sqrt{5})\right]$$

$$= \frac{1}{\sqrt{5}}\left[\frac{1}{2}(47 - 47 + 21\sqrt{5} + 21\sqrt{5})\right]$$

$$= 21$$

10

n	ϕ^n	ψ^n	L_n	F_n
1	1.618 034	−0.618 034	1	1
2	2.618 034	0.381 966	3	1
3	4.236 068	−0.236 068	4	2
4	6.854 102	0.145 898	7	3
5	11.090 170	−0.090 170	11	5
6	17.944 272	0.055 728	18	8
7	29.034 442	−0.034 442	29	13
8	46.978 714	0.021 286	47	21

As n increases, ψ^n becomes numerically smaller and oscillates between positive and negative values.

11 $\quad \dfrac{L_n}{L_{n-1}}$ 3, 1.333, 1.75, 1.571, 1.636, 1.611, 1.621 . . .

$\dfrac{F_n}{F_{n-1}}$ 1, 2, 1.5, 1.667, 1.6, 1.625, 1.615 . . .

Both ratios get closer to the golden ratio, because that is the ratio of successive terms given by the approximate formulas in both cases.

Handling inequalities

1 (a) From the graphs, $t + 3 > 5$ when $t > 2$.

(b) (i) $t = 4 \Rightarrow t + 3 = 4 + 3 = 7 > 5$, hence statement ① is true.

(ii)

t	-5	-4	-3	-2	-1	0	1	2	3	4	5
$t + 3$	-2	-1	0	1	2	3	4	5	6	7	8
$>5?$	No	No	No	No	No	No	No	No	Yes	Yes	Yes

(iii) The solution set for ① is $t > 2$.

2 (a) If $x - 4 > -3$ then $x > 1$.   (b) If $4x > 12$ then $x > 3$.

3 (a) If $-3x > 6$ then $x < -2$.

(b) When dividing or multiplying an inequality by a negative number, the inequality sign must be reversed.

(c) (i) The solution is correct.

(ii) $-3, -4, -5, \ldots$ $-2.1, -2.2, -2.3 \ldots$ etc.

(d) The two graphs cross at $x = -2$. When $x < -2$ the graph of $y = 5x + 1$ is below the graph of $y = 2x - 5$.

4 (a)
$$5x + 1 < 2x + 7$$
$$\Rightarrow \quad 3x < 6$$
$$\Rightarrow \quad x < 2$$

(b)
$$2x - 1 > 5 - x$$
$$\Rightarrow \quad 3x > 6$$
$$\Rightarrow \quad x > 2$$

(c)
$$1 - 2x < x - 7$$
$$\Rightarrow \quad 8 < 3x$$
$$\Rightarrow \quad \tfrac{8}{3} < x$$
$$\Rightarrow \quad x > \tfrac{8}{3}$$

(d)
$$3 > 1 + 2x$$
$$\Rightarrow 2 > 2x$$
$$\Rightarrow 1 > x$$
$$\Rightarrow x < 1$$

(e)
$$1 - \tfrac{1}{3}x < 4$$
$$\Rightarrow \quad -\tfrac{1}{3}x < 3$$
$$\Rightarrow \quad x > -9$$

(f)
$$3 - 2x > 2 - 3x$$
$$\Rightarrow \quad x > -1$$

Expanding brackets

1 (a) $x^3 - 1$

(b) $x(x^2 + 2x + 4) - 2(x^2 + 2x + 4) = x^3 + 2x^2 + 4x - 2x^2 - 4x - 8$
$$= x^3 - 8$$

(c) $x^3 + 1$

(d) $x^3 + 8$

2 (a) $(x + 1)(x^2 - 2x - 8) = x^3 - x^2 - 10x - 8$

(b) $(x - 2)(x^2 - 7x + 12) = x^3 - 7x^2 + 12x - 2x^2 + 14x - 24$
$$= x^3 - 9x^2 + 26x - 24$$

(c) $(x - 1)(x^2 + 6x + 5) = x^3 + 5x^2 - x - 5$

(d) $(x^2 - 2x + 1)(x + 3) = x^3 - 2x^2 + x + 3x^2 - 6x + 3$
$$= x^3 + x^2 - 5x + 3$$

3 (a) $(x^2 - 1)(x^2 - 4) = x^4 - 5x^2 + 4$

(b) $(x^2 - 4)^2 = x^4 - 8x^2 + 16$

(c) $(x - 1)(x + 3)(x^2 + 6x + 9) = (x^2 + 2x - 3)(x^2 + 6x + 9)$
$$= x^4 + 6x^3 + 9x^2 + 2x^3 + 12x^2 + 18x - 3x^2 - 18x - 27$$
$$= x^4 + 8x^3 + 18x^2 - 27$$

(d) $(x + 1)(x - 2)(x^2 - x - 12) = (x + 1)(x^3 - 3x^2 - 10x + 24)$
$$= x^4 - 2x^3 - 13x^2 + 14x + 24$$

Factorising polynomials

1 (a) (i) -24 (ii) -30 (iii) -24 (iv) 0

      (v) 0 (vi) 6 (vii) 0 (viii) -24

    (b) $x + 1, x + 3, x - 4$

    (c) $(x + 1)(x + 3)(x - 4) = (x^2 + 4x + 3)(x - 4)$
$$= x^3 - 13x - 12$$

2 (a) $a = -2$. The value is chosen so that $x + 2 = 0$.

    (b) $P(-2) = 0$, therefore $x + 2$ is a factor of $P(x)$.

3 (a) $P(2) = (2 - 2)(2^2 - 2 - 2) = 0$

    (b) $P(a) = (a - a) Q(a) = 0 \times Q(a) = 0$

4 $(x - 3)(x - 1)(x + 1)$ since $P(3) = 0, P(1) = 0, P(-1) = 0$

5 (a) $x^3 + 2x^2 - 9x - 18$

    (b) $x^3 + 5x^2 + 2x - 8$

6 $30 = 5a \implies a = 6$

7 (a) $P(x) = x^3 - bx^2 + 2x + x^2 - bx + 2$
$$= x^3 + (1 - b)x^2 + (2 - b)x + 2$$

    Like terms are gathered together to simplify the expression.

    (b) For the two expressions to be equal, the coefficients for each term must be the same. This is clearly true for x^3 and $+2$, also

$$1 - b = -2 \quad ① \quad \text{(from } x^2 \text{ term)}$$
$$2 - b = -1 \quad ② \quad \text{(from } x \text{ term).}$$

    The two equations both give $b = 3$.

    The process of obtaining equations from equivalent expressions by comparing coefficients is usually referred to as **equating coefficients**.

8 (a) $b = 2$; $(x - 1)(x - 1)(x + 3)$

    (b) $b = -2$; $(x - 7)(x - 4)(x + 2)$

9 (a) (i) $a = 1$ \
   (ii) $c = -4$ } These are easy to spot because only two terms are combined to give the particular term.

(b) $(x + 2)(x^2 + bx - 4) = x^3 + bx^2 - 4x + 2x^2 + 2bx - 8$
$$= x^3 + (2 + b)x^2 + (2b - 4)x - 8$$

Equating coefficients gives

$$2 + b = -1 \quad ①$$
$$2b - 4 = -10 \quad ②$$

Both equations give $b = -3$.

(c) $P(x) = (x + 2)(x^2 - 3x - 4)$
$P(x) = (x + 2)(x - 4)(x + 1)$

With practice it is possible to complete the stage represented by (b) entirely in one's head by doing it in logical steps. For example:

1. For the x^2 term,

   $(x + 2)(x^2 + bx - 4)$ gives $(2 + b)x^2$

2. $2 + b$ has to be -1, hence $b = -3$.

3. Check in the same way that this value gives -10 for the coefficient of x.

10 (a) $(x - 2)(x^2 + 11x + 24) = (x - 2)(x + 3)(x + 8)$

(b) $(x - 3)(x^2 + 1)$; does not factorise further.

5 Numerical methods

5.1 The golden ratio

How could you use a graph sketching package to solve

$2^x = 5?$

Either sketch the graphs of $y = 2^x$ and $y = 5$ and note where they cross

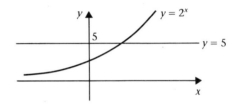

or sketch the graph of $y = 2^x - 5$ and note where it crosses the x-axis.

In either case, 'zooming-in' on the root will give greater accuracy.

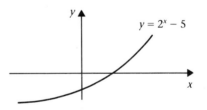

5.2 Locating roots

(a) In each arrangement

   (i) what graphs should you draw?

   (ii) which points give the solutions?

(b) Sketch the graphs and find bounds for the roots.

(c) Use the 'zoom' facility of a graph plotter to find the roots to 3 decimal places. Help is given on technology datasheet: *Zoom.*

(d) What are the advantages and disadvantages of the two arrangements?

(a) For $x^2 = x + 1$, draw the graphs $y = x^2$ and $y = x + 1$. The
solutions are at the points of intersection of the two graphs.

For $x^2 - x - 1 = 0$, draw the graph of $y = x^2 - x - 1$. The
solutions are the points where the graph cuts the x-axis.

(b) *Either*

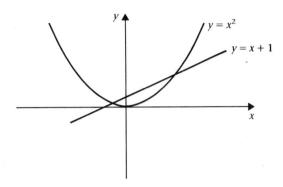

or

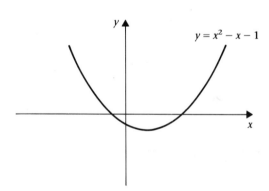

One root lies between -1 and 0. The second root lies between
1 and 2.

(c) The roots are -0.618 and 1.618.

(d) Without a graph plotter, $x^2 = x + 1$ gives two simple graphs to
sketch, but care must be taken to ensure that *all* solutions are
obtained. Note that approximate roots of *any* quadratic
equation can be found by sketching $y = x^2$ and a straight line.

With $x^2 - x - 1 = 0$ it is simple to check that no solutions have
been missed, but it is not so easy to sketch the graph without a
graph plotter.

5.3 Iterative formulas

> (a) Find x_4.
>
> (b) Continue to find x_5, x_6, x_7 etc. until you are confident that you know the solution to 3 decimal places. How can you decide when to stop?
>
> (c) In writing out your solutions, how many decimal places is it sensible to give for your intermediate results?

(a), (b) $x_4 = 3.1890\,(58\,983)$
$x_5 = 3.1916\,(60\,311)$
$x_6 = 3.1923\,(41\,14)$
$x_7 = 3.1925\,(19\,281)$
$x_8 = 3.1925\,(65\,889)$
$x_9 = 3.1925\,(78\,083)$

So the solution is 3.193 to 3 decimal places.
You can stop when two successive terms agree to this degree of accuracy.

(c) There is little point in recording more than 4 decimal places if only 3 are required in the final answer.

The golden ratio

1 The larger rectangle is an enlargement of the smaller by a factor of ϕ. Thus the longer side of the larger rectangle is ϕ times the longer side of the smaller rectangle, i.e. $\phi + 1 = \phi \times \phi$.

2 Since the sign changes between 1.6 and 1.7 the graph must have crossed the x-axis as shown in the diagram.

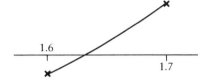

3 One way to speed up the method is to estimate from the function values the most likely interval. Since the value is -0.04 at $x = 1.6$ and 0.19 at $x = 1.7$, the solution is likely to be nearer 1.6 than 1.7.

The process could also be speeded up by dividing the interval into two and calculating the function value at 1.65 first. Once this is known, it will only be necessary to search one half of the interval. You could continue to halve the interval at each stage — this more efficient process is known as **binary search**.

4 $\dfrac{u_5}{u_4} = \dfrac{5}{3} \approx 1.667.$

5 $x_2 = \sqrt{x_1 + 1} = \sqrt{1 + 1} = \sqrt{2} = 1.414\,213\,6$

6 The 2.236 068 could in fact represent any number between 2.236 067 5 and 2.236 068 5. The error associated with it is therefore $\pm\,0.000\,000\,5$.

Iterative formulas

(a) $2x^2 = 5x - 1$

$$x^2 = \frac{5x-1}{2}$$

$$x = \sqrt{\frac{5x-1}{2}}$$

(b) $5x = 2x^2 + 1$

$$x = \frac{1 + 2x^2}{5}$$

(c) $2x^2 = 5x - 1$

$$2x = 5 - \frac{1}{x}$$

$$x = \frac{1}{2}\left(5 - \frac{1}{x}\right)$$

(d) $5x - 2x^2 = 1$

$$x(5 - 2x) = 1$$

$$x = \frac{1}{5 - 2x}$$

(e) Not possible

(f) $2x^2 - 4x - x + 1 = 0$

$$2x^2 - 4x + 1 = x$$

(g) Not possible

(h) Not possible

(i) $2x^2 = 5x - 1$

$$x^2 = 5x - 1 - x^2$$

$$x = \sqrt{5x - 1 - x^2}$$

(j) As is the case for several of the other formulas, it is easier to demonstrate correctness in reverse.

$$x - 2 = \sqrt{\frac{7 - 3x}{2}}$$

$$(x - 2)^2 = \frac{7 - 3x}{2}$$

$$x^2 - 4x + 4 = \frac{7 - 3x}{2}$$

$$2x^2 - 8x + 8 = 7 - 3x$$

$$2x^2 - 5x + 1 = 0$$